Pouran Jinchi

Published by **Akkadia Press 2019**

Akkadia Press
28 Forth Street
Edinburgh EH1 3LH
United Kingdom
www.akkadiapress.uk.com

Co-published with **Works on Paper**

Works on Paper
PO Box 72036, Dubai
UAE
www.thethirdline.com

الخط الثـــالث
the third line

The Third Line's book publishing division *Works on Paper* documents the work of contemporary Middle Eastern artists and seeks to increase their reach regionally and internationally.

To date, published books include the following: *Presence*, featuring the works of Emirati photographer Lamya Gargash with Arabic and English editions (2008); *In Absentia: Photographs by Tarek Al-Ghoussein*, printed in English and Arabic (2009); the self-titled treatise *Huda Lutfi* about the Egyptian artist's Cairo based practice (2010); *Cosmic Geometry*, an extensive monograph on Monir Shahroudy Farmanfarmaian, edited by Hans Ulrich Obrist and Karen Marta (2011) and the first monograph on the multidisciplinary practice of Canadian-Iranian artist Abbas Akhavan.

Managing Editor
Saira Ansari

Editor
Laura Egerton

Design and Layout
Omar Mismar

Printed and bound in Dubai by **Oriental Press**

ISBN 978-0-9956890-9-1

Table of Contents

Acknowledgements

The artist would like to thank the following people for their help and support during the making of this publication.

Anne Renahan
Ben Eastham
Claudia Cellini
Ladan Akbarnia
Laura Egerton
Maryam Ekhtiar
Omar Mismar
Rasheed ∵
Saira Ansari
Scott Cantini
Shiva Balaghi
Sunny Rahbar
My family

Introduction

It is with great pleasure that Works on Paper presents the first monograph on the nearly 25-year-long art practice of Pouran Jinchi. The self-titled publication follows the artist's prolific career, examining work produced across varied media, and helps to reimagine the engagement of Persian calligraphy within a contemporary art discourse.

Jinchi's work has been exhibited across the world in solo and group presentations and is housed in important institutional collections across the USA and UAE, and globally. It has been at the forefront of our work at The Third Line to help contextualize Jinchi's practice through the many historical and contemporaneous concepts and issues that it references. The depth of these conceptual trajectories can be fully understood by navigating Jinchi's interest in language, history, politics and religion, and through the literary works that have deeply affected her manner of thinking and making.

We are indebted to our contributors, who agreed to be a part of this project and helped create a resourceful dialogue around Jinchi's practice and the evolution of contemporary calligraphy. This publication would not have been possible without the invaluable commentaries of Dr. Maryam Ekhtiar (Associate Curator, Department of Islamic Art, Metropolitan Museum of Art, New York), Dr. Shiva Balaghi (independent scholar) and Ben Eastham (writer, founding editor of *The White Review* and Associate Editor of *ArtReview*). Between Ekhtiar and Balaghi, these observations range from the academic, to the historic, and finally to the intimate—excavating the personal and social constructs that inform Jinchi's work. While Ekhtiar and Balaghi are both familiar with Jinchi's practice and are well-versed in the vocabulary of Persian calligraphy, Eastham has the unique perspective of approaching the visual language and its corresponding texts as an exercise in exploring the influence of literature on artists and, specifically, its resonance in Jinchi's work.

We worked closely with Jinchi, and designer and artist Omar Mismar, to produce a book that embodies Jinchi's aesthetic and illustrates the content through a rich palette of visuals. The challenges of revisiting earlier work—much of which lacked proper documentation—prompted the unearthing of works packed away in archives, and photographing them to help complete the study. The process, spread across nearly a year, reinforced why Jinchi's work has always been so special to us. It is our hope that this publication will enrich the reader's knowledge of Jinchi's practice and provide an important resource material that will stay relevant for years to come.

Sunny Rahbar
Co-founder, The Third Line

What Is Good Somehow Remains

Shiva Balaghi

Snow piles against the windows of her Brooklyn studio as Pouran Jinchi bends over a table, drawing in the grey winter light. As she works, a radio tuned to National Public Radio plays the news. It's been a hectic few months of tending to practicalities, all the tangential work of being an artist. Jinchi feels the need to immerse herself in making art. The immediacy of drawing suits her mood. "It's very intimate, drawing," she says. "At the same time, it can be very powerful."[1]

Her latest series is linear drawings made of graphite pigment on colorfix paper. They have a modernist sensibility, studies in geometric abstraction. But as one moves closer into the work, shapes of saturated color give way to hundreds of precisely drawn thin lines that merge into an intricate pattern. On the surface, the work appears to be purely a formal intervention, a study on linearity, perspective and color. The drawings are a play on grids,

Whiskey (The Line of March series), 2016
Graphite on colorfix paper
19.5 × 19.5 inches

1   Unless otherwise noted, all quotations from Pouran Jinchi are from interviews and correspondence with the author.

variations on a theme, each echoing a similar composition, with two larger fields intersected by a colorful line that disrupts the asymmetricality of the page. The series shares a palette of muted rust and mauve, blue and olive, grey and black, intercepted with bright red and yellow. A detailed glimpse shows that each drawing is actually created from a variety of colors, lines merging into patterns, blending together to create unexpected effects. The work underlines the gentle power of repetition rendered in detailed precision. "Up close, these drawings are delicate and frail. Depending on how you look at them, they can convey both vulnerability and strength," Jinchi tells me.

What appears to be a purely formal experiment in design and color is actually steeped in Jinchi's interest in military aesthetics. The drawings are based on signal flags used by navies as they traverse international waters. "Each signal flag," Jinchi explains, "depicts geometric shapes that correlate to letters. So, though they look different, each of the drawings in this series spells out the word 'No' using the codes of signal flags."

On the face of it, the drawings may seem a departure for Jinchi. But in fundamental ways, they reflect key inclinations that characterize her approach to making art—a constant formal experimentation, a mining of the interplay between the textual and the visual, and a preoccupation with the balance of beauty and pain. Jinchi is a meticulous planner. With each new body of work, she creates detailed sketches. Her studio becomes something like a workshop—scraps of metal, smears of paint, strips of paper. The discovery of materiality is central to Jinchi's process. Perhaps this stems from her background in math and sciences; she trained as a civil engineer at university.

Jinchi's art practice takes shape through a dynamic synergy between deeply researched concepts and a constantly evolving formal approach. Her art is

The Red Line (detail), 2017
Copper, brass and enamel paint
198 pieces, various sizes

characterized by an unconventional use of materials and an unexpected use of color. All of it works together—technique, material, color, exhibition design—to visually translate a particular set of ideas. When she begins to make the pieces, the careful planning can fade away. Control gives way to spontaneity, order gives way to impulsive gestures. A generative contrast between rigid precision and fluid movement has become a hallmark of her art.

For the past several years, Jinchi has been working with copper and brass, making of the metals a canvas onto which she paints, or manipulating them into sculptural form. This process of experimentation culminated in her sculptural installation, *The Red Line*. This is a game of chess-cum-battle, inspired by an archival photograph

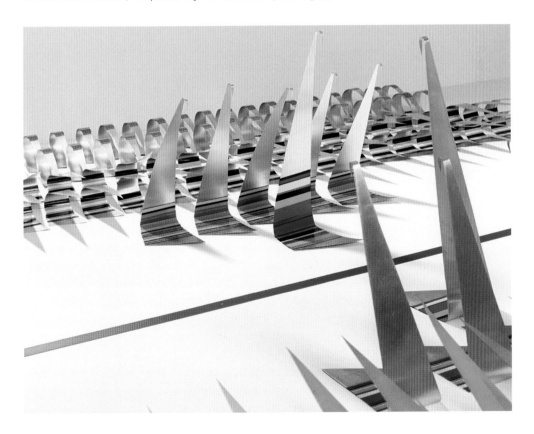

Jinchi came across from 1920s Leningrad, showing Soviet chess masters playing the game at the Palace Square using soldiers from the Red Army as the black pieces and sailors from the navy as the white pieces. Jinchi created dozens of metal objects, each painted with bright stripes suggesting military ribbons. Some stand at full attention, others bend forward; each is labeled with its rank—pawn, rook, knight. As she worked on the sculptures, Jinchi wanted to better understand the ways the metals, as organic matter, would react with the elements. She consulted expert conservators and, following several meetings and a series of tests, she received a rather lengthy and detailed scientific report. She poured over the study with fascination and began testing new methods for preserving her metalwork.

What Jinchi uses to make her art reflects the underlying ethos of each piece. For her Alef series, shown as part of the *Tarjama/Translation* exhibition at the Queens Museum of Art in 2009, Jinchi reworked Elmer's glue to reinvent the look of traditional Islamic tile work. She turned Lucite into a kind of paper, painstakingly writing the Quran by hand onto sheet after sheet. Layering the translucent pages with light, she created her iconic *Rose Quran*, now in the permanent collection of New York's Pratt Institute. The surface reflects the substance of the artworks.

Jinchi's use of color is somewhat idiosyncratic. Some works are rendered in shades of grey, black and white; others in bold saturated hues of greens, pinks and blues. Always, the use of color is deliberate. For each series, Jinchi creates a new color palette. Sometimes she blends custom colors and she intermittently uses acrylic, ink, car paint and lacquer for various effects. "I use color in my art as a way to convey meaning," she explains. For her 2017 exhibition, *The Line of March*, held at The Third Line, Dubai, Jinchi used primary colors taken from military insignia and naval flags, and khakis echoing desert camouflage.

Jinchi has had a longstanding interest in military linguistics—Morse code, naval flag signals, the NATO phonetic alphabet. The latest manifestation can be seen in her recent "No" drawings. They tap into Jinchi's larger interest in the ways language can be used to reveal and obscure, clarify and obfuscate. Language and the arts as parallel modes of communication is a central conceptual concern for Jinchi. An examination of the intersectionality of the visual and the textual, the relationship between what can be seen and what can be said, is present in some manner in nearly all of her artworks, going back to her earliest paintings from the 1990s inspired by the poetry of Omar Khayyam.

"Artists," she explains, "always use their art to say something they cannot convey with words." This interplay between the written word and the image is central to Jinchi's art. "I use text, words, letters, literature and poetry in my art. For me, the challenge is always this—how to get the viewer to experience the written words through a visual sensory. It's a different kind of sensory. We are used to reading with our eyes and grasping meaning with our minds. I try to communicate between the space where words are seen and visuals are experienced. It's a kind of storytelling."

For some years, Sadegh Hedayat's modernist novel, *The Blind Owl*, has fueled Jinchi's imagination. Written in the interwar period, the novel deals with creative angst during times of social upheaval and political violence. In a central passage, the book's narrator proclaims: "I write only for my shadow, which is cast on the wall in front of the light. I must introduce myself to it." In a series of paintings, drawings and sculptures, Jinchi inscribed, altered and reassembled the literary classic. She painted the words onto raw canvases, obsessively repeating the letters over and over again until calligraphic order gives way to colorful abstraction. The textual landscapes in vivid hues of fuchsia, purple and red evoke a battlefield strewn with rubble.

With *Hanged*, Jinchi recast calligraphic painting into sculptural form, giving shape to the first page of the novel. She painstakingly dismantled the text, cutting each letter from a sheet of copper, forming it into curvular shapes, and then stringing the letters onto a chain fabricated from copper safety pins. Hanging alongside one another, the sculptures sway gently, catching the light and casting shadows on the wall. "The play of light and shadows is very much by design," Jinchi explains. "There's the artwork itself and then its shadow cast on the wall." This interplay between form and content, between the sculptures and their shadows, parallels the structure of Hedayat's novel that revolves around the central character's dialogue with its own shadow. It's a telling reflection on the power and limits of art.

Jinchi is an avid reader, often taking breaks from working to read in her studio. She's a habitual reader of *The New York Times* and magazines like *The New Yorker* and *The Atlantic*. I ask Jinchi about her proclivity to listen to the news as she makes art in her studio. "Unlike many other artists, I don't listen to music while I'm working," she explains. "I need another dimension, something beyond pleasure." This steady stream of news often detailing violent world events—trenchant wars, political revolutions, devastating earthquakes, raging wildfires—all of it seeps into her artworks.

Jinchi's aesthetic sensibility emerges from a quiet dissonance, a heady tension between beauty and violence. Underpinning her art is an ongoing preoccupation: what is the role of the artist amidst turmoil and conflict? Increasingly, this quest has turned to a reckoning with seemingly perpetual violence that leaves behind continuously unfolding and deeply painful consequences. Creativity becomes a way of remembering and manifesting, of bearing witness to what may seem incomprehensible. "We are surrounded by so much violence in contemporary society," she explains, "that we have almost grown numb."

Hanged (Black and Blue series), 2015
Copper, paint and safety pins
18 strands, approximately 7 × 34 inches each

In 2001, Jinchi executed a number of calligraphic paintings she refers to as the Derakht/Tree series. In *Derakht 11*, Persian letters, recognizable yet illegible, tumble organically to form the silhouette of a tree with leaves scattering around its roots. *Derakht 8* is a study in linear abstraction, a close-up of branches dangling down, their shadows reflecting across the canvas. In *Derakht 14*, the branches of the tree are formed by jumbles of letters, with some perfectly calligraphed letters suspended as though floating leaves falling from the tree. Here, one begins to discern letters and diacritical notations, recognizing that the letters that constitute the paintings spell out *derakht*, the Persian word for tree. There is a subtle distinction between the recognizable and the legible, between what can be seen and what can be comprehended.

The paintings are somber, rendered in acrylic and ink in greys and blacks against a stark background that suggests a barren sky. There is nothing overtly political in the paintings, but they are a response to a heady moment. Sometime after the attacks of September 11, 2001, Jinchi was driving from New York to the beach in Long Island for a necessary escape. From the window of the car, she saw a grove of trees that had burned. For her, this image of the charred trees came to represent the sense of devastation of the recent tragedy. The paintings speak of mourning and loss. They reflect a mood rather than codifying a readily legible visual politics. And they are utterly beautiful paintings.

"Beauty," says Jinchi, "is very important to me. Of course it can be very subjective. But I am very visually sensitive. When I encounter something beautiful, it makes me feel calm. I actually feel a physical response, a spark in my eyes that then reverberates to all my other senses." For Jinchi, beauty produces an effect; it becomes a communicative modality between her as the artist and the viewer seeing her work.

Beauty in Jinchi's art is an enticement to look. When our field of vision becomes saturated with violence, the temptation is to avert our gaze. Jinchi's art offers a respite, a middle space, somewhere between complete disconnection and total immersion. Looking at her artworks is a contemplative, sometimes even meditative, experience. A moment of reprieve that lets us focus on grids of lines, curves of letters, shapes of saturated color. But those expressive gestures hold meaning. And though she would rarely be counted as a political artist, hers is perhaps an art that is suited to the politics of our time.

These days we hear that people are experiencing "political fatigue." When the news seems to be a steady stream of disturbing violence, there is a natural impulse to turn off the news, look away, and disconnect. "I cannot tune out,"

Untitled 11 (Derakht series), 2001
Ink and acrylic on canvas
72 × 60 inches

Jinchi explains. "For me, to tune out creates anxiety." Instead, even as Jinchi inscribes turmoil into her art, she balances it with attention to intricately constructed surfaces. Beauty in Jinchi's art creates an opening, carries its message through a visual experience. Her politics veers away from the didactic and ideological to that which stimulates the viewer's own reflection and engagement. The theorist Jacques Rancière wrote, "Art should allow us to be absorbed in our thoughts, to distance ourselves, to have a moment of rest."[2] If it may seem that Jinchi's art offers such respite, it ultimately serves as a prompt, a way to absorb the impact of the unbearable through a more gentle sensual experience.

The illegibility of the politics—sometimes driven by a particular event, other times a reflection of a more general mood—is intentional. The task of seeing, of deciphering and reacting is ultimately left to the viewer. "The beauty in my art is ultimately a hopeful sign, that even in times of utter destruction, what is good somehow remains. The hope that even through the fog of war, we can somehow find our way back to what is beautiful."[3] In one of his most enduring essays, "The White Bird," the critic John Berger wrote, "The problem is that you can't talk about aesthetics without talking about the principle of hope and the existence of evil."[4]

I check back in with Jinchi. The New York snow has melted into rain. She's propped open the door to her studio, letting in some fresh air. From time to time, she looks up from her desk and watches the droplets of rain stream across the window. As the radio plays the day's news, she works on another signal flag drawing. "Two letters," she tells me, "N and O. This one is on a deep blue paper; the lines are red and yellow."

We 2 (Two Letter Words series), 2018
Mixed media
27.5 × 19.75 inches

Overleaf
Victor (The Line of March series), 2016
Graphite paper
19 × 18.5 inches

2 "The Politics of Art: An Interview with Jacques Rancière," *Verso Blog*, (November 9, 2015), https://www.versobooks.com/blogs/2320-the-politics-of-art-an-interview-with-jacques-ranciere

3 "Scripts and Sensibility: Iranian-American Pouran Jinchi," Interview with Lisa Pollman, *Art Radar* (05/09/2016), http://artradarjournal.com/2016/09/05/scripts-and-sensibility-iranian-american-pouran-jinchi-interview/

4 John Berger, "The White Bird," in *The Sense of Sight* (New York: Vintage Books, 1985), p. 5.

'WE', 2018   Pemma Smith

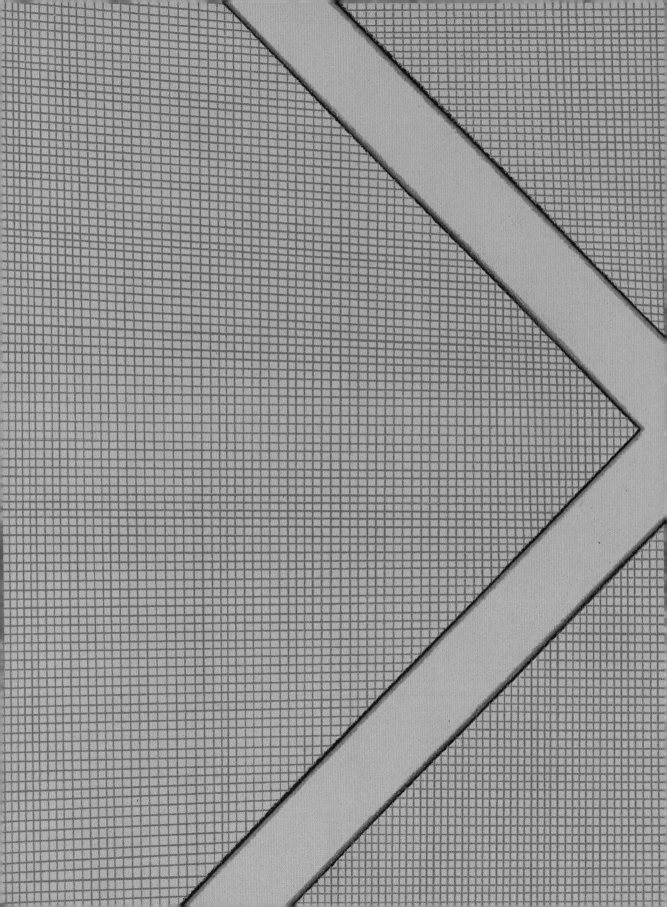

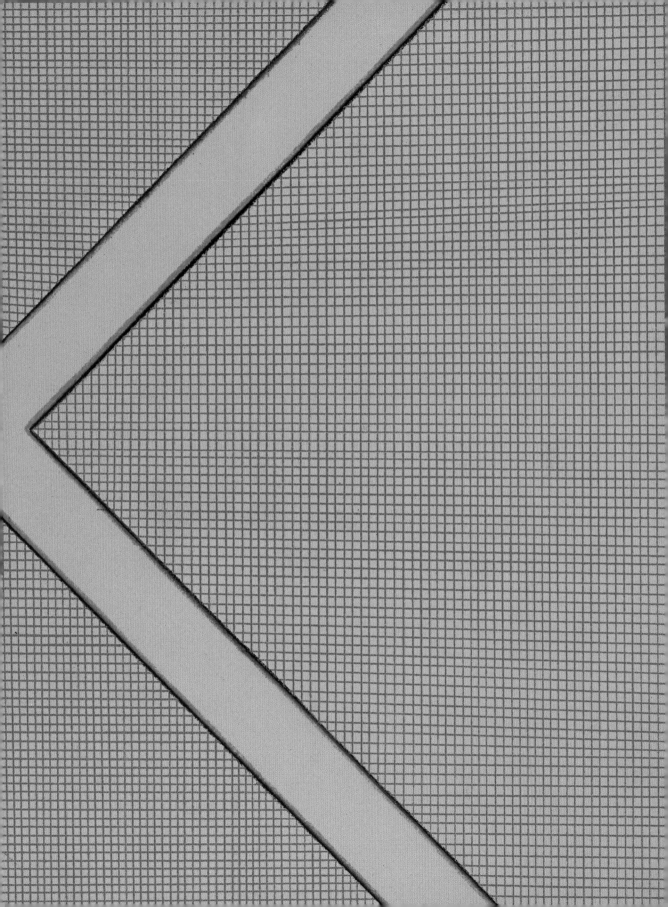

Signs
and Ciphers

Maryam Ekhtiar

Pouran Jinchi has been exploring the art of calligraphic abstraction and its polysemic associations since the beginning of her artistic career. She has drawn on the versatility, malleability and creative possibilities of the forms of the letters of the Persian alphabet to create a compelling and vibrant visual language of her own. Trained as a traditional calligrapher in Iran, it is no surprise that she has chosen *nasta'liq*, long regarded as the bride of scripts and the visual essence of the Persian language as her script of choice. *Nasta'liq* is known for its lyricism and fluidity of movement, rendering it the quintessential script of Persian poetry (See image p. 22). For Jinchi, the letters are not only signifiers of sound or meaning, but also forms with a life and energy of their own. By focusing on a select group of works from various stages of her career, this essay will follow the evolution of her multivalent and rich practice.

Untitled 95 (Rubaiyat series), 1995
Mixed media on canvas paper
9 × 12 inches

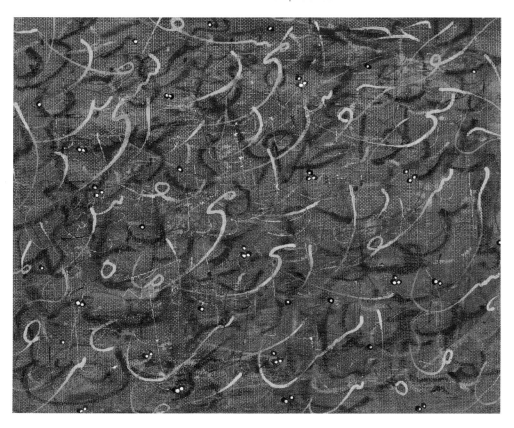

Like other artists who have embraced minimalism and calligraphic abstraction as their preferred form of visual expression, in her work Jinchi has straddled the boundaries of word and image, legible and illegible and writing and picturing. Her early works are more literal. In these, she uses verses of Persian poetry by classical poets such as Omar Khayyam (1048–1131) or Hafez (1048–1131) as a springboard, although she renders the actual verses unrecognizable through a process of layering, juxtaposing and fragmenting the letters. She deconstructs the verses, breaking them down, reducing and representing them in fresh and innovative compositions. One example is a dense cluster of words and letters in *nasta'liq* over which she incises a scrawled layer of illegible writing (See image p. 21). The contrast between the well-formed letters and the incised scribbles introduces a striking tension of binaries.

The concept of underlying energy is a key force in Jinchi's work, one that is consistently present throughout her practice. Her works resonate with nature's pulses in subtle and mysterious ways. Whether repeating themselves in a rhythmic march, floating weightlessly on the surface of the canvas, swirling like a cyclone or piled on top of one another, the letters and diacritical marks are infused with life. Many of her compositions are asymmetrical with large areas of empty space; the letters are clustered in one corner of the canvas with a few letters struggling to break free. The Murcheh series reveals her childhood fascination with ant colonies and the distinct manner in which large numbers of ants congregate and move. Jinchi uses the letters that make up the Persian word for ant (*murcheh*) and explores the correlation between the shapes of the bodies of the ants and the letters of the word to reconstruct this natural phenomenon. Here, the energy is slow-moving and restrained. The ants function collectively as they cluster together and meander across the canvas (See image p. 23).

In the Entropy series, Jinchi presents a different kind of energy—one that is vigorous and driven by a powerful

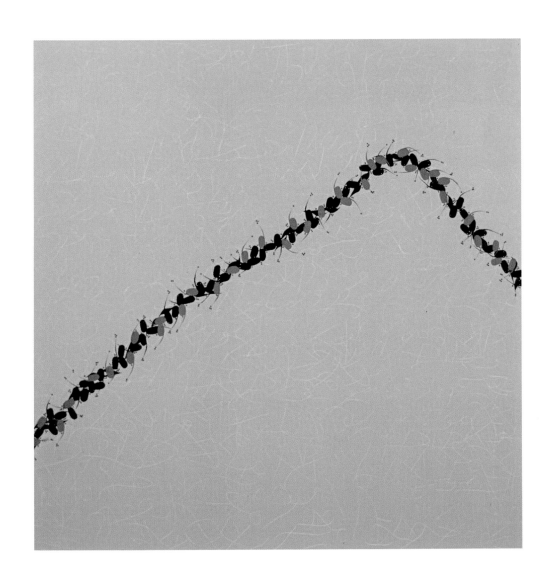

centripetal, centrifugal or magnetic force. The composition of the letters vacillates between chaos and order and often builds up to a crescendo (See image p. 25). In this series she uses a striking palette of dark blue and green that intensifies the effect of the underlying energy embodied in the work. The closest counterpart to these calligraphic works is the traditional *siyah mashq* or calligraphic practice pages executed by calligraphers and scribes. These consist of irregular, undulating and overlapping repetitions of individual letters, groups of letters or words. The original purpose of *mashq* was to strengthen a calligrapher's hand, perfect the shapes of the letters according to an intended model and instill focus and discipline. These works were an integral part of a calligrapher's practice. Prized for their compositional qualities, *siyah mashq* gained popularity in Iran and eventually became an art form in its own right. Folios were widely collected from the 17th century onwards and were often given lavish borders and placed into albums alongside paintings, drawings and calligraphic specimens (See image p. 24). Jinchi also looks west to the works of American artists such as Mark Tobey (1890–1976) and Brice Marden (b. 1938) who in turn referenced East Asian calligraphy as a source of energy and spirituality. In Jinchi's works, process is key. Her tools and implements are integral to her practice. Rather than using the traditional reed pen, she renders her compositions with special metal pens of various widths that correspond to the intended scale of the script and overall composition.

Throughout her career, Jinchi has engaged with the semiotic dimensions of calligraphic abstraction, highlighting the complex relationship between sign, form and meaning. In the series Tajvid, she omits the consonants and pens the vowel marks (diacriticals), *sura* titles and numerical markings of a selection of *Quranic* verses onto a long scroll. Here, she explores the notion of *tajvid*, the rules governing pronunciation in recitation of the *Quran*. Since vocalization and diacritical marks traditionally functioned as aids to the

correct pronunciation of the verses, Jinchi celebrates these often overlooked auxiliary markings rather than the actual letters (See images p. 25 and 27). In a later series, Alef paintings, in artworks *Virgool* and *Saaken,* she draws on the same concept. The panels consist of the embossed letter *alef*, diacriticals and punctuation marks such as the *saaken* (pause-mark) and the comma or quotation mark. By foregrounding these and giving them pride of place, she challenges the conventional traditions of reading the text, offering creative alternatives and approaches.

The series Dawn, Noon and Night looks at the performative and meditative aspects of the Muslim ritual prayer (*salat*). *Salat*, one of the key pillars of Islam, is performed five times a day and involves four different postures. Here, Jinchi focuses on prostration, in which the forehead along with the palms and knees of the worshipper touch the ground in submission. She uses the *mohr*, a tablet made of baked clay, symbolizing earth or soil from the holy cities of Mecca, Kerbala and Najaf, as her medium of expression. Used in ritual prayer primarily by Shi'ite believers, the *mohr* is typically placed on the spot where the worshipper's forehead meets the ground when praying. Since she was born and raised in the holy city of Mashhad in Northeastern Iran, home to the sacred shrine of Imam Reza, she grew up collecting these prayer tablets.

These works are made by rubbing wax charcoal on Japanese Okawara paper over the embossed inscriptions and decorative motifs on the surfaces of a selection of disc-shaped *mohr*. The inscriptions usually include the word Allah, as well as invocations to religious personages. Jinchi then outlines the forms with pencil to delineate the details and rich texture of the imprints. The repetition, rhythm and layout of the forms on white or black paper imbue these works with a distinct aesthetic and a unique meditative quality akin to the act of prayer itself. One example, *Noon 1* in the collection of the Metropolitan Museum of Art, features small circular imprints of the

mohr repeated and superimposed to form a cross (See image p. 29). The circles are all the same size, with the exception of the one at the center, which is the largest. Here, the repetition of the text, markings and gestures makes for a mesmerizing overall composition.

Jinchi has long been absorbed by the interplay between text and image and art and literature, probing yet another facet of the semiotic potentials of calligraphic abstraction. This time, she has focused on the internationally acclaimed, psycho-fiction short story, *The Blind Owl* by the writer Sadegh Hedayat (1903–1951). Hedayat, long considered the father of Iranian modern prose, wrote this controversial novella in 1936 but did not publish it in Iran until 1941. It has been banned in Iran several times since its release and is still banned for its provocative content. Like the Czech writer Franz Kafka (1883–1924) or the American Edgar Alan Poe (1809–1849), Hedayat was a satirist and social critic of his time (Iran in the 40's and 50's) whose preoccupation with pain, suffering and death is a recurring theme in his writings.

In several consecutive series, Jinchi examines various aspects of the *The Blind Owl*. In Pierced she uses the following quote from the short story as a point of departure: "I write only for my shadow, which is cast on the wall in front of the light. I must introduce myself to it." She explains: "Each word of the quote is fragmented, hacked, pierced, and disembodied. I then stitched the letters together but out of order, rendering them unreadable. To me piercing is a way of inflicting pain in order to adorn the body." In *Blind Owl* (Pattern), Jinchi creates 71 pieces representing the same number of letters as present in the quote. Using pen and copper on paper, she draws out individual letters and embellishes them with decorative tattoo-like patterns, once again alluding to the act of inflicting pain as a means of creating beauty and asserting individuality. Similarly, in *The Blind Owl* (Dot series) she creates 96 drawings represented by the dots of the letters rather than the letters themselves, each corresponding to one of the 96 pages of the book, while in the Hammered and Hanged series (2014) she decodes elements from the story into sculptural forms hammered into copper plates, or painstakingly cuts out copper letters to create 18 strands of hanging sculptural forms that contain the words of the first page of the short story. Her use of hues of shiny copper and red accentuate the delicate balance between beauty and violence. In these series, she deconstructs and represents Hedayat's text and ends up reinterpreting it and creating her own personal narrative. These works facilitate an ongoing dialogue with a masterpiece of modern Iranian literature that speaks poignantly of pain and a fear of death as a universal reality.

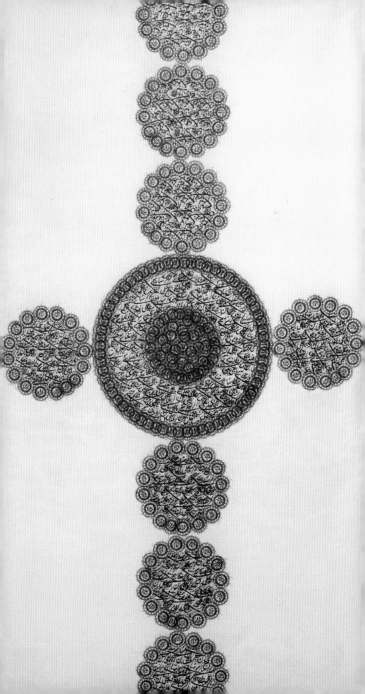

Since the beginning of her artistic career, Jinchi has been drawn to the overlap and interplay between form, language, sign, meaning and spirituality. She never ceases to explore new territories and experiment with new materials. Her works, which started out as mainly oil on canvas or board, have expanded into so many other media. The journey continues as she marries sign and design, art and literature, and translates her fascination with nature's mysterious forces and her memories, emotions and responses to moments of despair and crisis into visual form.

This Silence Is a Language Which We Do Not Understand[1]

Ben Eastham

1   See Sadegh Hedayat, *The Blind Owl*, trans. D.P. Costello (New York: Grove/Atlantic, 2010), 35.

A statement made "in black and white" brooks no dissent. "Purple prose" or "silver speech" is not to be taken seriously, while "plain speaking" is a reliable indicator of authority. The "blunt" truth is "unadorned" and never "decorative," so "smooth talk" and "pretty words" should arouse suspicion. "Clarity" is to be admired over "obscurity," to which the proper response is skepticism. Respect is due to "hard" facts and "weighty" assertions, disdain to "soft" or "airy" opinions. If the language of power is monochrome, masculine and unambiguous, then the language of resistance is colorful, feminine and polysemous. Pouran Jinchi belongs, with the poets, firmly in the latter camp.

Her paintings, etchings and sculptures invest letters and words with colors and forms that delight the senses and compromise conventional legibility. *A as Alpha Green* (2017) transforms part of a calligraphic mark into a grid of glossy tiles describing a brightly colored pattern resembling a musical score. By incorporating a fragment of the Persian alphabet into so visually stimulating an arrangement, the work challenges the assumption that our reading of language can ever be divorced from our sensory experience of it.

This intensely visual representation of a single glyph brought to mind Vladimir Nabokov's description of the synaesthesia that meant he experienced letters and words as colors and textures:

> The long "a" of the English alphabet has for me the tint of weathered wood, but the French "a" evokes polished ebony. This black group also includes hard "g" (vulcanized rubber) and "r" (a sooty rag being ripped). Oatmeal "n," noodle-limp "l," and the ivory-backed hand mirror of an "o" take care of the whites. I am puzzled by my French "on" which I see as the brimming tension-surface of alcohol in a small glass.[2]

2   Vladimir Nabokov, *Speak, Memory* (London: Penguin Classics, 2000), 34.

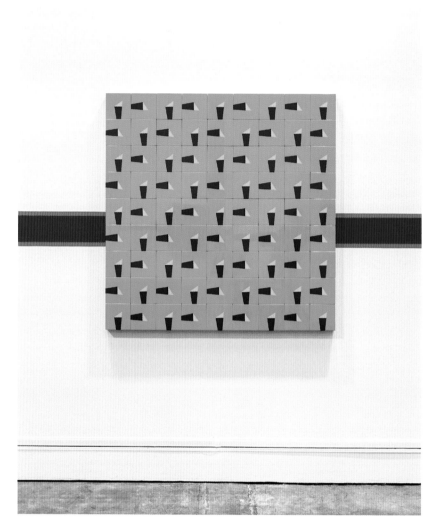

For Nabokov, for anyone attuned to language there is no such thing as a plain statement in black and white. Words are always endowed with sensory properties, and are subject to the same personal and secret mythology that governs our individual aesthetic preferences.[3] Each of us find certain words attractive to the ear and others repellent,

3   A relevant example being recent research that suggests synesthestes match letters and colors according to the alphabet block toys they used as children. Nabokov's synesthetic wife Nora assigned different colors to the same letters because of cultural differences in their childhoods.

and we respond (whether consciously or not) to the patterns that lines form when laid out on the page. These are the nuances of language that conventional language suppresses in the name of legibility, and that poetry exploits.

The stitched-together symbols of Jinchi's Black and Blue series brought to mind Ezra Pound's description in "In a Station of the Metro" of "faces in a crowd" as "petals on a wet, black bough".[4] Both depend on a kind of fractured collage technique that asks the reader to fill in the gaps; the whole defined as much by what is absent as what can be seen. Neither makes conventional sense—the more you try to apply logic to Pound's juxtaposition of a Japanese idyll with a Parisian train station, the less effective it becomes, while Jinchi's abstracted symbols have no fixed independent meaning—but that only enhances their power. Like poems—designed to be spoken aloud and seen on the page—the drawings entangle idea, sound and image to the point that they cannot function independently.

Both Pound and Jinchi also take inspiration from works in another medium—Pound drawing on an Ukiyo-e print he had seen in the British Museum, Jinchi from Sadegh Hedayet's *The Blind Owl*—and seek connections between the two. This similarity extends to their formal presentation. In its original printed form, long stretches of white space separate phrases in Pound's poem, resembling the same minimalist grid into which Jinchi organizes her orphaned symbols.

As a poem is made to be spoken as well as seen—the series of sharp consonants falling at the end of Pound's line into the pillowing softness of "bough" means that its effects cannot be divorced from its sounds—so Jinchi's pictures sometimes demand to be spoken aloud. I frequently find myself imagining what works like *Entropy*

A as Alpha Green (The Line of March series),
Installation view at The Third Line, Dubai, 2016
Enamel on MDF panels
54 × 54 inches

4   Ezra Pound, "In a Station of the Metro," in *Poetry* (Chicago, April 1913).

#16 (2011)—with its dramatic mise-en-page—might sound like. (In the "private language," that Nabokov wrote, a rainbow would be transcribed as "kzspygv"; my attempts to vocalize Jinchi's work are no more pronounceable.)

This multimodal combination of textual, aural, tactile and visual elements has a precedent in concrete poetry and the calligrammes of Guillaume Apollinaire. As the words of "Il Pleut" (1914) are arranged on the page so as to resemble raindrops running down a windowpane, so

Jinchi paints the letterforms that make up the word for "ant" (*murcheh*) as an army of tiny black shapes swarming over the canvas. Paintings in which the component parts of language collapse into piles or arrange themselves into columns also recall Ian Hamilton Finlay's early experiments with the page as a visual field. To the properties of poems—at once pictures to be looked at, words to be delivered and codes to be deciphered—Jinchi adds touch.

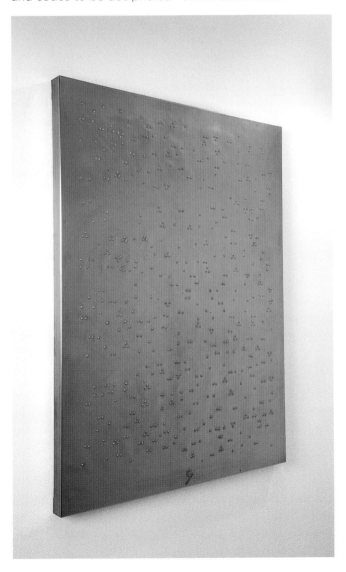

The embossed copper panel of *Hammered 3* (2014), for instance, reproduces the diacritics from a single page of *The Blind Owl*. The decision to efface the Persian text, leaving only the abstract patterns created by these shallow indentations punched by hand into the metal, might initially be understood as an oblique commentary on the continued censorship of the book in Jinchi's native Iran. Yet these repeated marks also read like Braille, a form of communication encoded in the topography of a material and interpreted through the fingers.

The effect is to makes Hedayat's *Blind Owl* at once more and less accessible to its audience. In the obvious sense, Jinchi renders the text unreadable by effacing all but the accents; yet she also universalizes the novel's sentiment by moving it outside and beyond written language. You do not need to read Persian to appreciate the shimmer of light across the copper's pockmarked surface, and by these means to engage with the text as it has been translated—in the broadest sense of the word—by Jinchi. *Hammered 3* strikes me as a fresh interpretation of the novel's prevailing themes of love, suffering and loss.

The work also has the aura of a devotional object, offering a physical link to a hallowed text (the artist first read *The Blind Owl* in her adolescence and has remained fascinated by it). By encoding words in touch it reminded me of the rosary beads I was encouraged to worry as a child, their passage through the fingers prompting my memory into reciting the prescribed phrases of penitence. This attraction to ritualized activity is equally apparent in Jinchi's series Bruised (2014), for which the artist copied out line after line of text, layering them until words, and by extension literal meanings, were lost. The works conjured not only *siyah mashq*, the practice sheets executed by apprentice scribes as part of their training in the art of calligraphy, but also the lines of scripture written out by misbehaving schoolchildren as punishment or the mantras recited in pursuit of altered states.

Bruised 2 (Black and Blue series), 2014
Transfer paper
18 × 18 inches

Bruised 1 (Black and Blue series), 2014
Transfer paper
18 × 18 inches

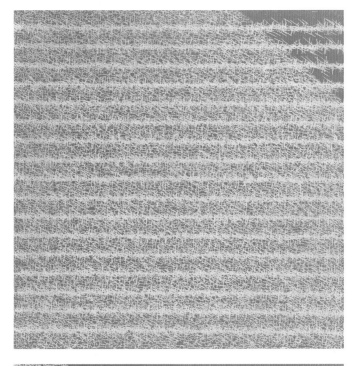

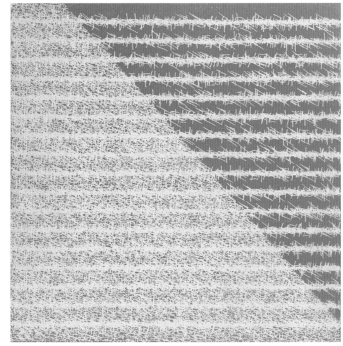

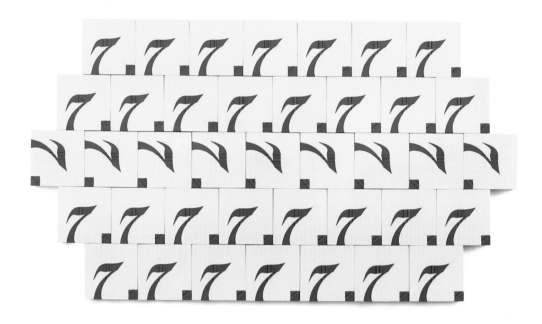

Bruised participates in the minimalist traditions of repetition, seriality and process. The emotive power of an approach sometimes misrepresented as drily academic is exemplified by Sol LeWitt's *Wall Drawing 46* (1970) which, like much of Jinchi's work, depends on the faithful execution of a simple set of rules. Originally effected two days after the death of LeWitt's close friend Eva Hesse (to whom the work is dedicated, and by whom its use of a "non-straight" line was inspired), the instructions for the wall drawing are as follows: "vertical lines, not straight, not touching, covering the wall evenly."[5] The laborious process of rendering these lines might be understood as an analogue for mourning, and the finished drawing closely resembles tears running down a face, Apollinaire's "Il Pleut" and—in the sense of encoded expression— numerous of Jinchi's etchings as well as her series of "Morse Code" embroideries.

5   Sol LeWitt, *Wall Drawing 46*, 1970. Black pencil. LeWitt Collection, Chester, Connecticut.

Those embroideries were included in the 2017 exhibition *The Line of March*, which also featured works deconstructing the international phonetic alphabet and rearranging its fragments into elaborate graphic patterns (including *A as Alpha Green*). These works further the artist's commitment to disrupting conventional boundaries, not only between image and text but also between high and low subjects, the discourse of power and the language of the outsider. Virginia Woolf railed against the fact that in a patriarchal society traditionally feminine pursuits such as fashion are dismissed as "trivial" in comparison to masculine preserves like sport. Those prejudices extend to the appraisal of art: the critic assumes, Woolf says in *A Room of One's Own*, that "this is an important book ... because it deals with war. This is an insignificant book because it deals with the feelings of women in a drawing-room."[6] By aestheticizing military codes to the point that they could hang in the most tasteful drawing room, works such as *J as Juliet* (2017) seem deliberately to "trivialize"—in Woolf's application of the word—and thereby to undermine the symbolic authority on which masculine power depends. By deconstructing the language of power—by sensualizing it—she exposes and defuses the violence embedded in it.

In her essay "The Laugh of Medusa," Hélène Cixous called for a literature that, through experimentation and playfulness, could subvert the dominant discourse of "plain" truths and "black-and-white" logic.[7] In psychoanalytic terms, it would operate in the realm of the real rather than the province of symbols, free from the constraints of conventional writing. Reluctant to define this new style of writing in a language already prejudiced against it, Cixous instead used metaphors: it should be sweet like honey, unstable like the ocean, nourishing like milk. Pouran Jinchi has created just such a language, at once private and universal, perfectly clear and defiantly obscure.

6   Virginia Woolf, *A Room of One's Own* (New York: Harcourt Brace, 1929), 128.
7   Hélène Cixous, "The Laugh of the Medusa," trans. Keith Cohen and Paula Cohen, in *Signs* Vol. 1, No. 4 (Summer, 1976), 875–893.

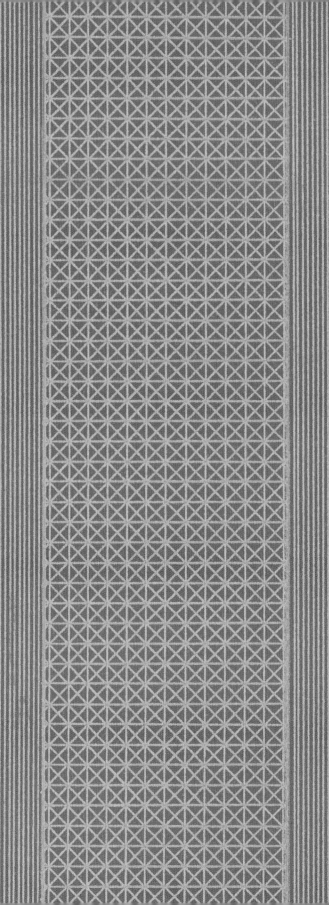

 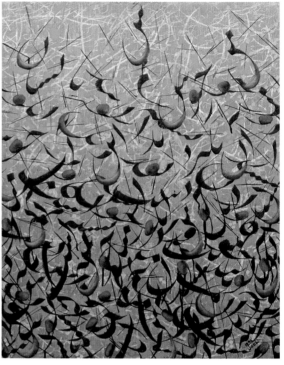

Above

Where the Love Thief Goes
(Poetry series), 1998
Mixed media
34 × 48 inches

Untitled 14 (Poetry series), 1996
Ink and acrylic on canvas
30 × 24 inches

Opposite

Untitled 5 (Poetry series), 1993
Mixed media
34 × 48 inches

Untitled 8 (Poetry series), 1994
Mixed media
34 × 48 inches

Untitled 1 (Rubaiyat series), 1995
Mixed media on canvas paper
9 × 12 inches

Untitled 10 (Rubaiyat series), 1995
Mixed media on canvas paper
9 × 12 inches

Untitled 25 (Rubaiyat series), 1996
Mixed media on canvas paper
9 × 12 inches

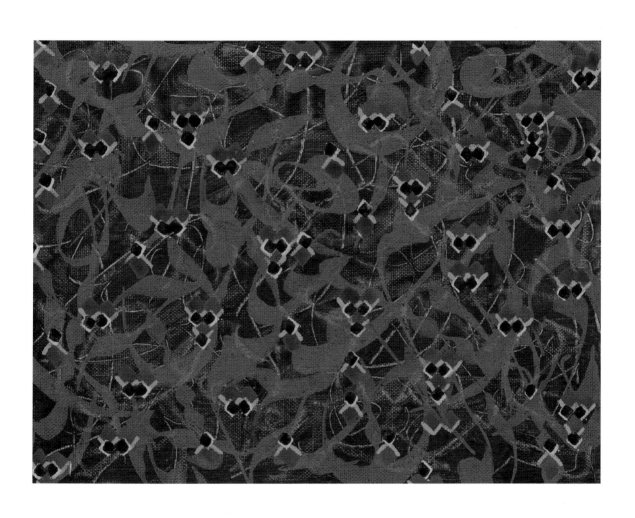

Untitled 29 (Rubaiyat series), 1996
Mixed media on canvas paper
9 × 12 inches

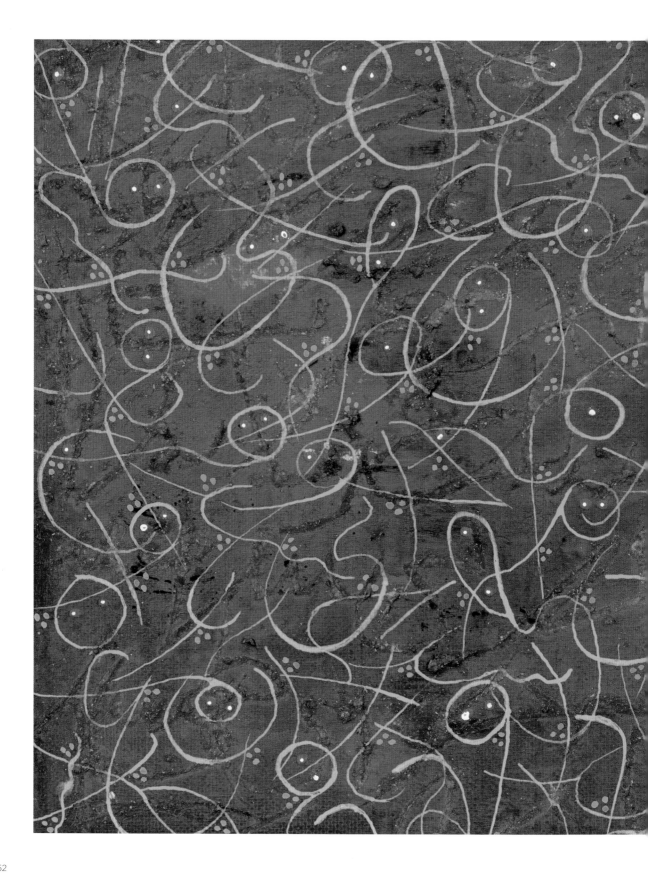

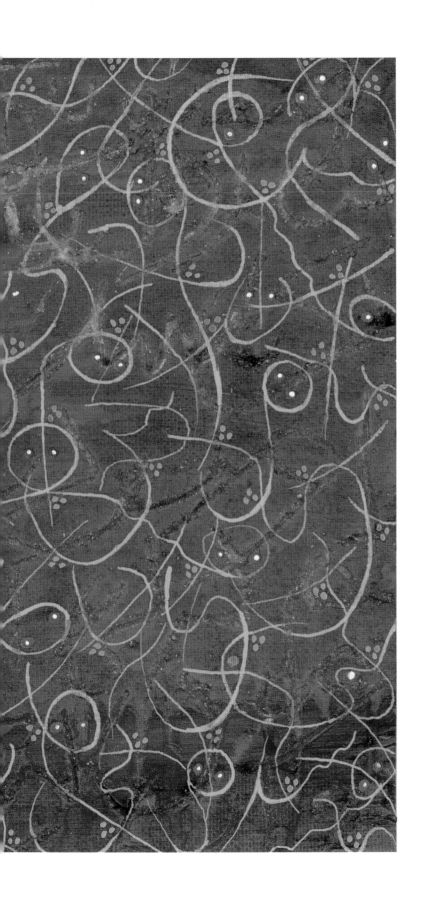

Untitled 63 (Rubaiyat series), 1996
Mixed media on canvas paper
9 × 12 inches

2/21   Jinchi, 1998

Untitled 2, 1998
Etching, 2 of 21
45 × 6 inches

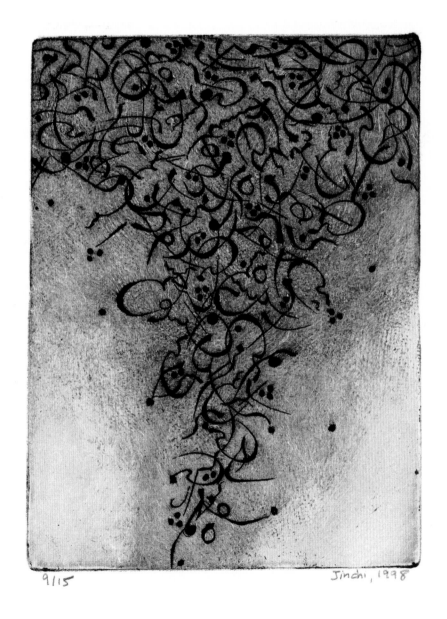

9/15   Jinchi, 1998

Untitled 1, 1998
Etching, 9 of 15
6 × 4.5 inches

Untitled 17 (Derakht series), 2003
Ink and acrylic on canvas
60 × 36 inches

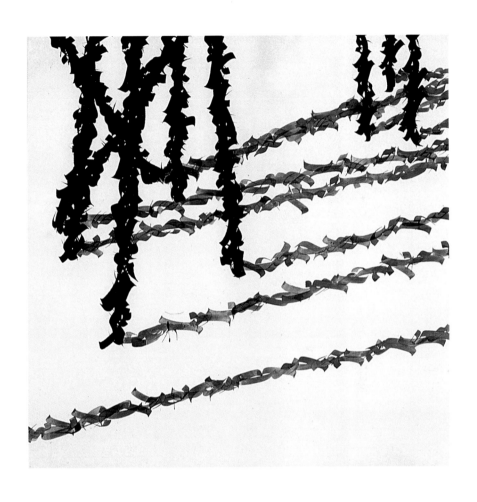

Untitled 8 (Derakht series), 2001
Ink and acrylic on canvas
48 × 48 inches

Above
Untitled 2 (Derakht series), 2002
Ink and acrylic on canvas
59 × 59 inches

Left
Untitled 1 (Derakht series), 2003
Ink and acrylic on canvas
59 × 59 inches

Opposite
Untitled 26 (Derakht series), 2002
Ink and acrylic on canvas
48 × 36 inches

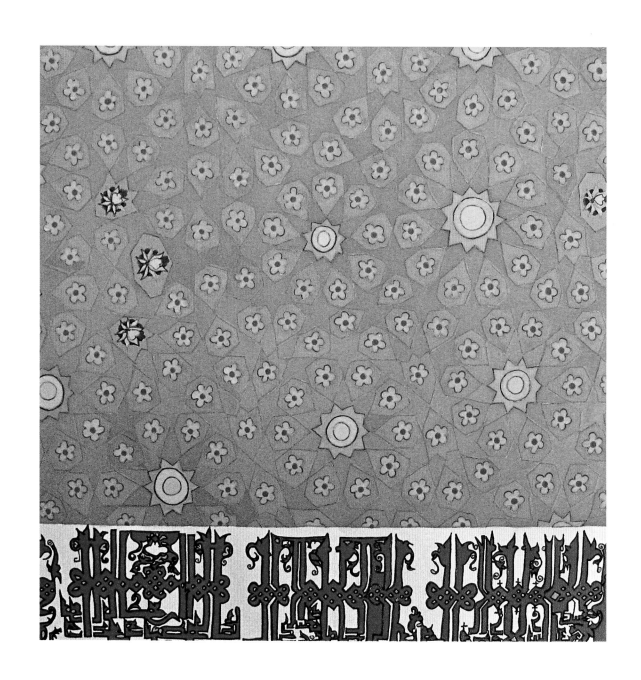

Pattern 1 (Fabricated series), 2007
Gouache on clayboard
12 × 12 inches

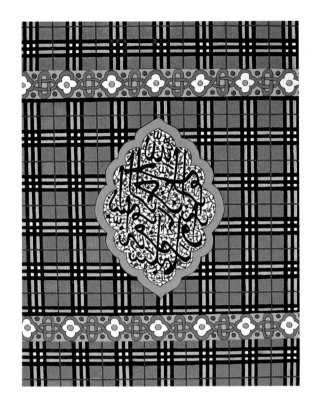

Clockwise from top left

Dual pattern 4, 3 and 1
(Fabricated series), 2007
Gouache on clayboard
14 × 11 inches

Above
Untitled 1 (Tile series), 1994
Acrylic on canvas
30 × 30 inches

Left
Untitled 2 (Tile series), 1994
Acrylic on canvas
30 × 30 inches

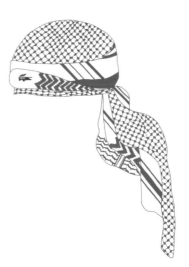

Above left

Headgear Louis Vuitton
(Fabricated series), 2005
Gouache on paper
30 × 23 inches

Above right

Headgear Lacoste
(Fabricated series), 2005
Gouache on paper
30 × 23 inches

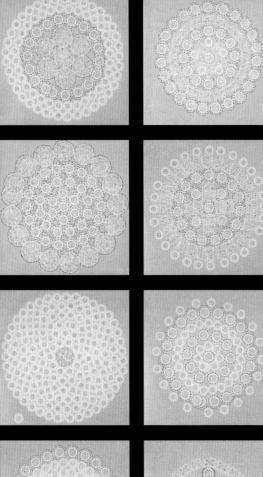

Left column, top to bottom
Morning 1, 2, 3, 4 and 5
(Ritual Imprint series), 2009
Charcoal and pencil on rice paper
18 × 18 inches

Right column, top to bottom
Morning 6, 7, 8, 11 and 12
(Ritual Imprint series), 2009
Charcoal and pencil on rice paper
18 × 18 inches

Opposite
Night 3
(Dawn, Noon and Night series), 201
Mixed media on Yatsuo paper
37 × 25 inches

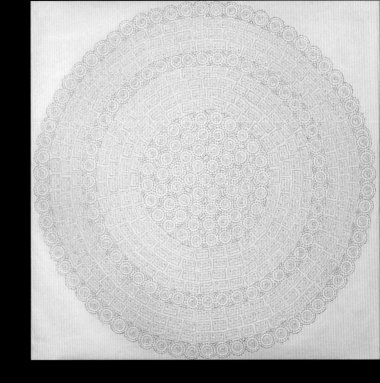

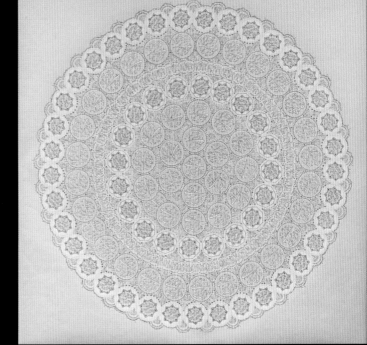

Noon 3 (Ritual Imprint series), 2012
Mixed media on Okawara paper
74 × 39 inches

Opposite
Noon 6
(Ritual Imprint series) (detail), 2010
Mixed media on Okawara paper
74 × 39 inches

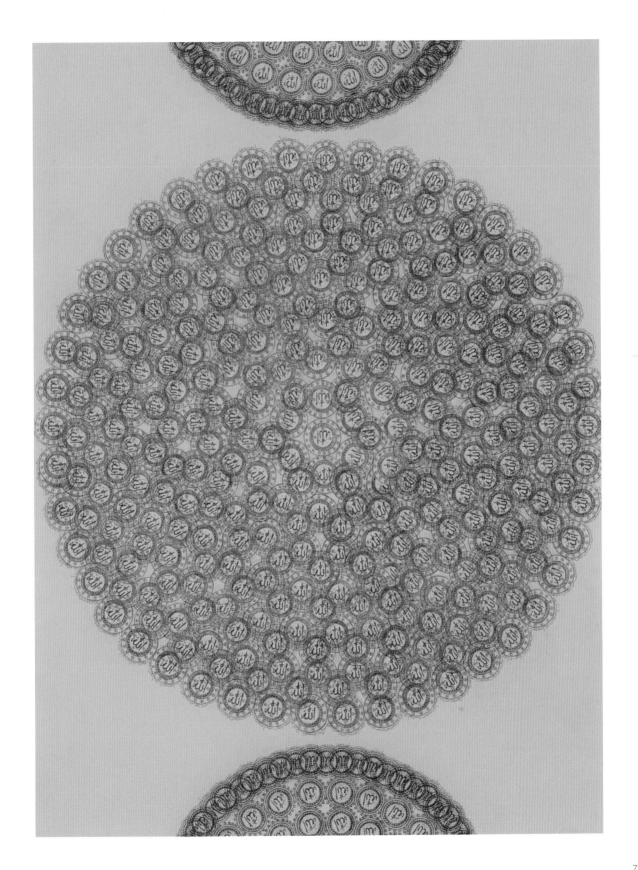

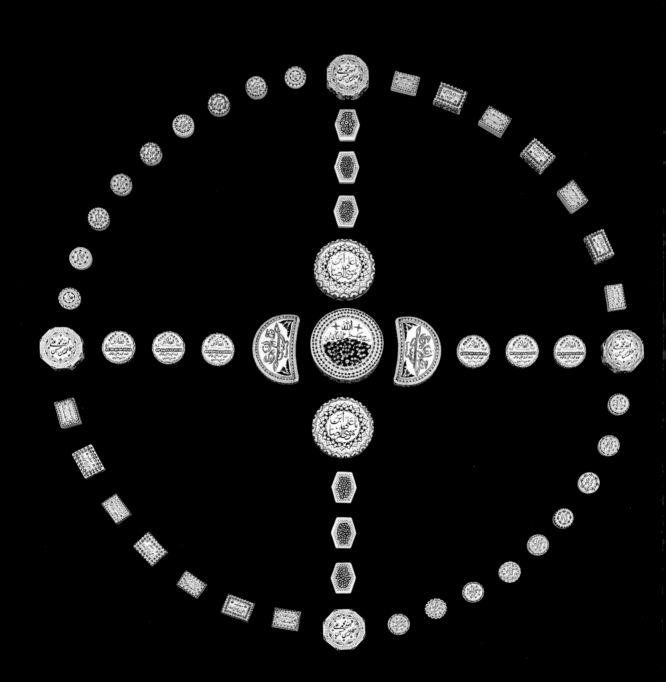

Untitled 14
(Entropy series) (detail), 2010
Ink and acrylic on canvas
48 × 36 inches

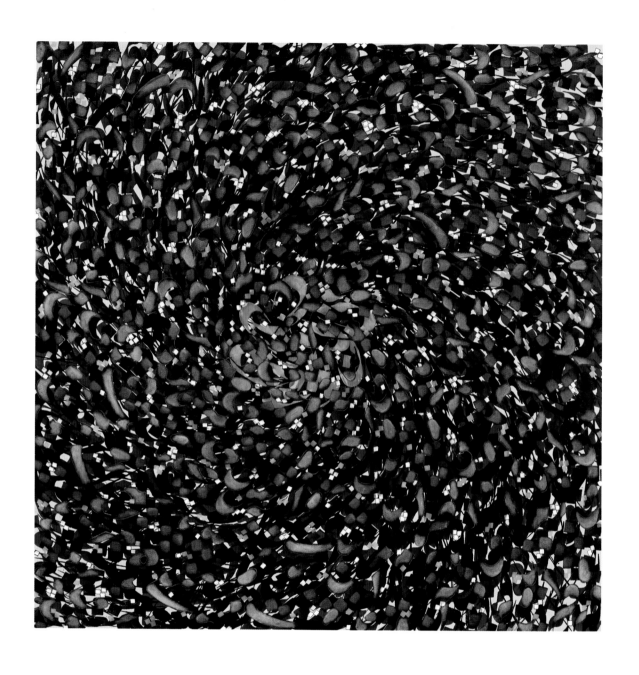

Untiled 3 (Entropy series), 2010
Ink and acrylic on canvas
48 × 48 inches

Untitled 6 (Entropy series), 2010
Mixed media on canvas
48 × 48 inches

Above left
Untitled 5 (Forough series), 2008
Ink and acrylic on canvas
60 × 48 inches

Above right
Untitled 3 (Forough series), 2008
Ink and acrylic on canvas
60 × 48 inches

Opposite
Untitled 4 (Forough series), 2008
Ink and acrylic on canvas
60 × 48 inches

Opposite
Untitled 18 (Transparency series), 2012
Plexiglas and permanent marker
4 × 3 inches

Above
Untitled 12 (Transparency series), 2012
Plexiglas and permanent marker
23 × 3 inches

Right
Untitled 16 (Transparency series), 2012
Plexiglas and permanent marker
6 × 2.5 inches

Overleaf
Untitled 1 (Transparency series), 2011
Plexiglass and permanent marker
36 × 36 inches

Transparency 2
(Transparency series) (detail), 2011
Plexiglass and permanent marker
15 pieces 72 × 6 inches each

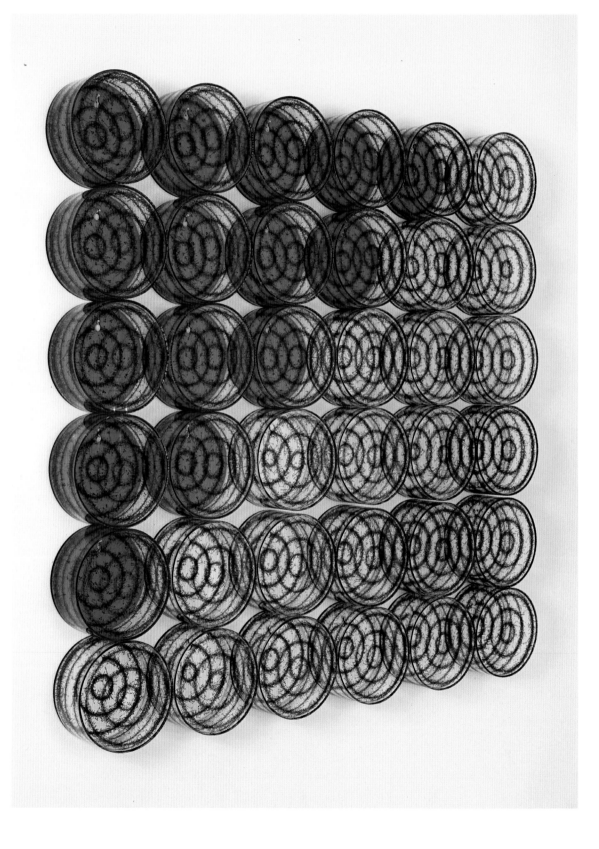

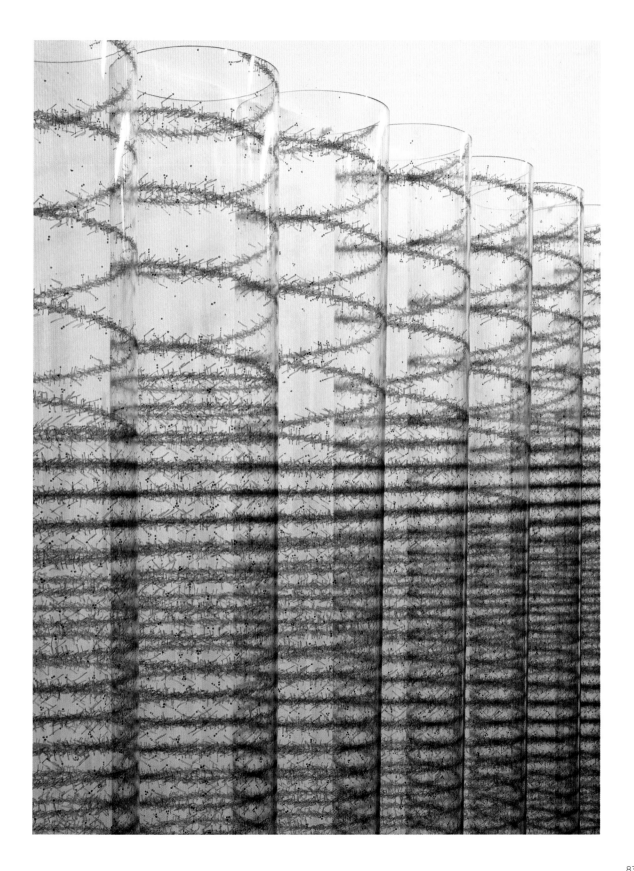

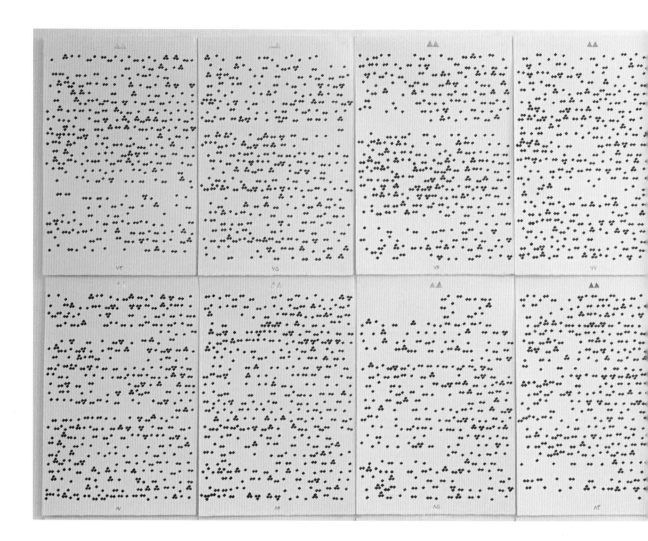

Dots (The Blind Owl series) (detail), 2013
Ink and copper on paper
95 pieces, 111 × 285 inches,
22.25 × 15 inches each

Opposite

Dots (The Blind Owl series)
Installation view at The Third Line,
Dubai, 2013

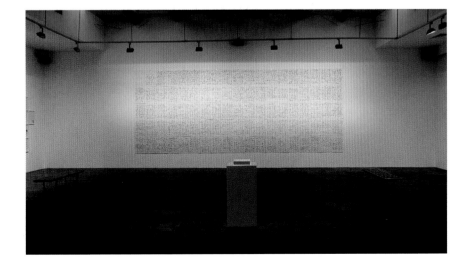

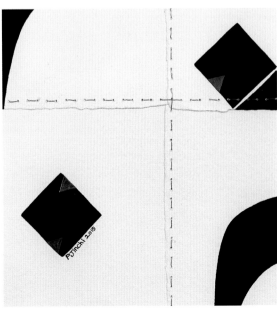

Opposite

Hammered 5
(Black and Blue series), 2014
Copper on panel
40 × 30 inches

Above

Stitched 2
(Black and Blue series), 2015
Ink, copper and copper thread on
handmade paper
52 × 47 inches

Right

Stitched 2 (detail), 2015
Ink, copper and copper thread on
handmade paper
52 × 47 inches

Foxtrot
(The Line of March series) (detail), 2016
Enamel on wood panels
81 pieces, 102 × 54 inches

Opposite
Foxtrot (The Line of March series), 2016
Enamel on wood panels
81 pieces, 102 × 54 inches

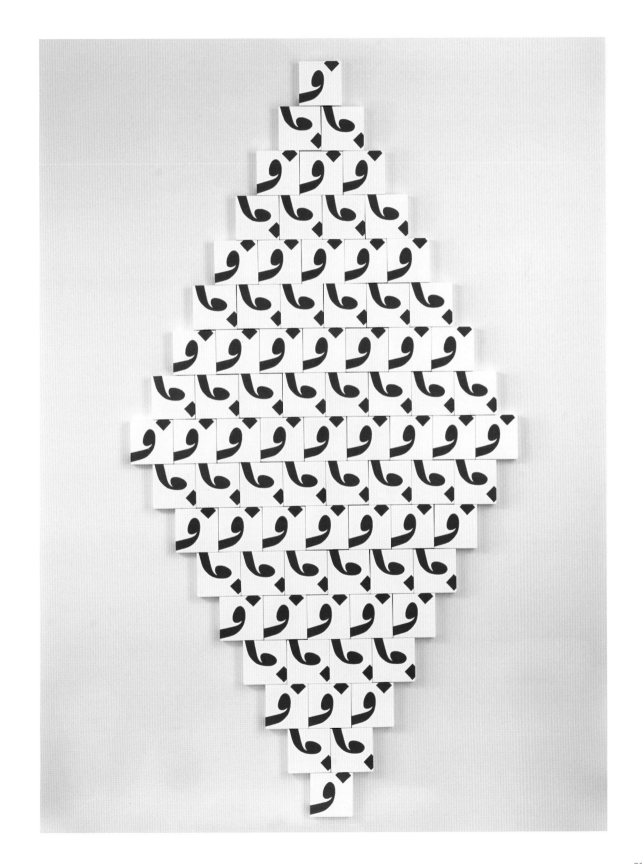

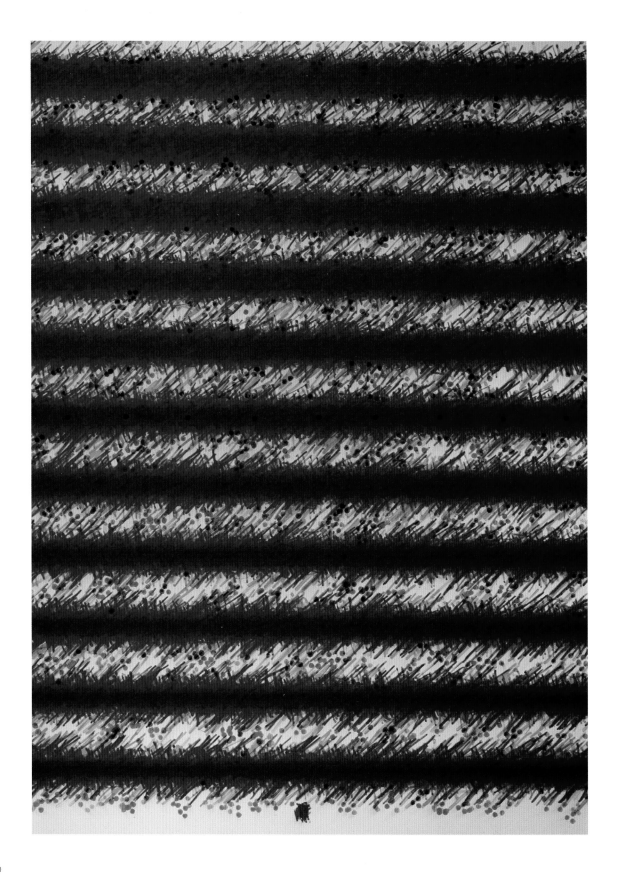

Untitled 2
(The Blind Owl series) (detail), 2013
Plexiglass, permanent marker, plinth
and light
10 × 12 × 2 1/8 inches

Untitled 2 (The Blind Owl series), 2013
Plexiglass, permanent marker, plinth
and light
10 × 12 × 2 1/8 inches

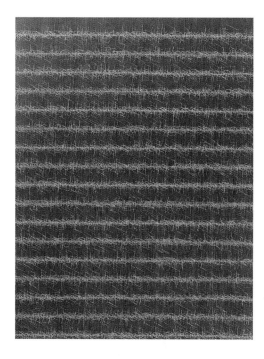

Clockwise from top left
Untitled 1 (The Blind Owl series), 2015
Scratched graphite paper
25 × 20 inches

Untitled 2 (The Blind Owl series), 2015
Scratched graphite paper
25 × 20 inches

Untitled 4
(The Blind Owl series) (detail), 2015
Scratched graphite paper
25 × 20 inches

The Rose Quran, 2013
Pens, paint, Plexiglass, light and plinth
18 × 18 × 15 inches

Overleaf
The Rose Quran (detail), 2013
Pens, paint, Plexiglass, light and plinth
18 × 18 × 15 inches

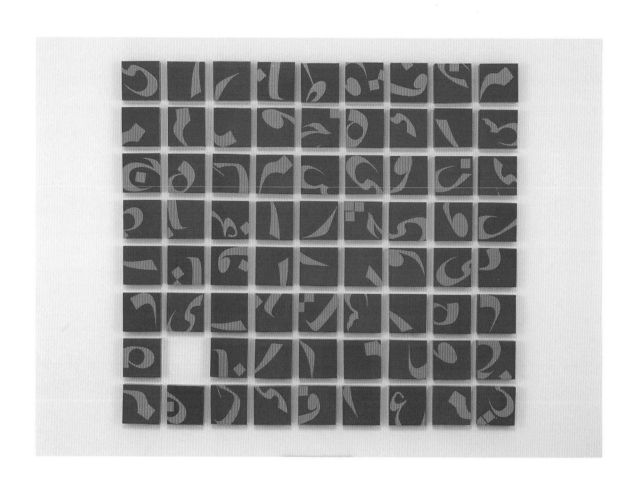

Hacked (Black and Blue series), 2014
Enamel on wood panels
55.5 × 63 inches

Slashed (Black and Blue series), 2014
Enamel on wood panels
62.25 × 77 inches

Untitled 3 (The Blind Owl series), 2013
Copper and paint
41 × 17 × 10 inches

Artist tools and materials

Hanged (Black and Blue series), 2015
Copper, paint and safety pins
17 strands, approximately 7 × 33 inches each

Opposite
Hanged (detail), 2015
Copper, paint and safety pins
17 strands, approximately 7 × 33 inches each

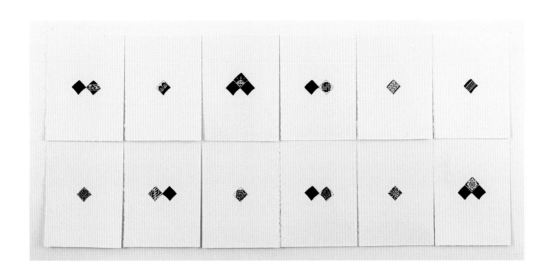

Opposite

Pierced (detail), 2014
Pens and copper thread on
handmade paper
36 × 108 inches

Above

Inked (Black and Blue series), 2014
Pens on paper
A group of 243 drawings.
15 × 11.25 inches each

Right

Inked (Black and Blue series), 2014
Pens on paper
A group of 243 drawings,
15 × 11.25 inches each

Above

Wound 1 (Black and Blue series), 2015
Inks on linen
48 × 48 inches

Left

Wound 2 (Black and Blue series), 2015
Inks on linen
48 × 48 inches

Opposite

Morse Code Red
(The Line of March series), 2017
Embroidery floss on linen
48 × 36 inches

M as Mike
(The Line of March series), 2016
Installation view at The Third Line,
Dubai, 2017
Enamel on MDF panels
54 × 42 inches

A as Alpha Blue
(The Line of March series), 2016
Enamel on MDF panels
54 × 54 inches

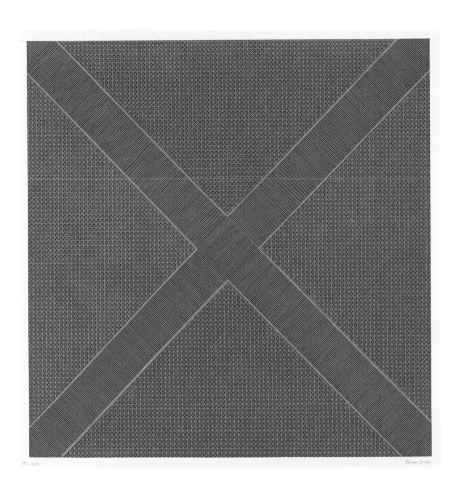

Mike (The Line of March series), 2016
Graphite on colorfix paper
19.5 × 19.5 inches

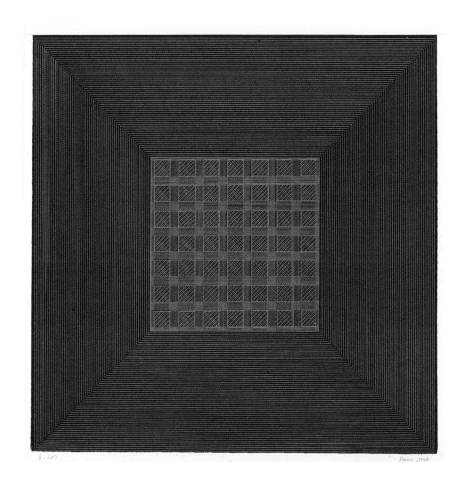

Sierra (The Line of March series), 2016
Graphite on colorfix paper
19.5 × 19.75 inches

Overleaf

The Line of March,
Installation view at The Third Line,
Dubai, 2017
A group of 18 signal flags
Approximately 60 × 180 inches

Above

The Line of March
Installation view at The Third Line,
Dubai, 2017

Opposite top

The Red Line
(The Line of March series), 2017
Copper, brass and enamel paint
198 pieces, various sizes

Opposite bottom

The Red Line
(The Line of March series) (details), 2017
Copper, brass and enamel paint
198 pieces, various sizes

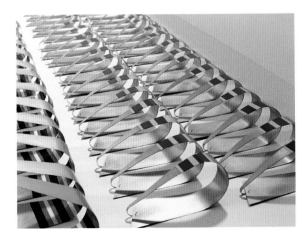
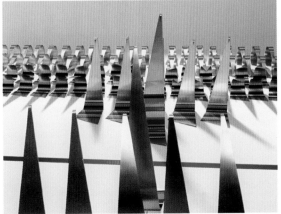

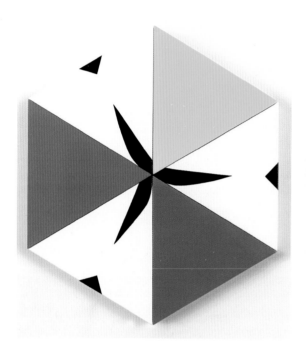

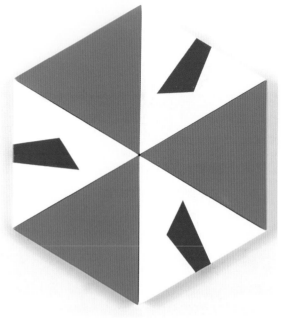

Clockwise from top left

Z as Zulu Hexagon
(The Line of March series), 2017
Enamel on MDF panels
18 × 15.5 inches

A as Alpha Hexagon
(The Line of March series), 2017
Enamel on MDF panels
18 × 15.5 inches

B as Bravo Octagon
(The Line of March series), 2017
Enamel on MDF panels
18 × 15.5 inches

Opposite, anticlockwise from top left

B as Bravo Hexagon
(The Line of March series), 2017
Enamel on MDF panels
18 × 15.5 inches

P as Papa Octagon
(The Line of March series), 2017
Enamel on MDF panels
18 × 15.5 inches

T as Tango Octagon
(The Line of March series), 2017
Enamel on MDF panels
18 × 15.5 inches

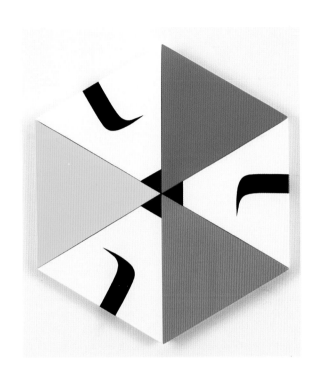

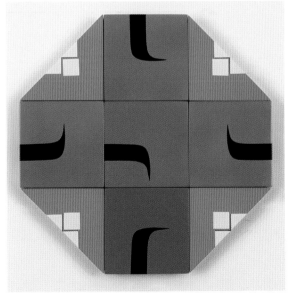

Artist Biography

Pouran Jinchi's artistic process thrives on a creative tension between control and chaos. Months of careful planning go into each of her series before she begins making art. From researching a concept through copious reading, to playing with pigments to derive just the right color, to testing the chemical reactions of materials, Jinchi delves into every detail when planning her artworks. Her research becomes a process of discovery, from medieval Persian poetry to archival photographs, from popular film to music. But on those days when she is in her studio, all of these fade into a quiet meditative space and making art becomes an immersive, ethereal experience. Jinchi's paintings, drawings and sculptures combine a meticulous craftsmanship with unexpected jolts that surface in these spontaneous moments of creation.

Her series function like chapters in a larger book. They are characterized by unique formal and technical qualities, but ultimately speak to larger meanings and relate to core issues Jinchi conveys in her art. What is the relationship between the artist and society? How can an art convey the intangible essence of an experience? What is the function of an artist in times of social upheaval and political turmoil? How do art and language function as modes of communication? Inevitably, these concerns are mediated with her unique life experiences and personal histories, which affect her art.

Born in Mashhad, a sacred shrine city in Iran, Jinchi became attuned early in life to the ways architecture, objects, decoration and the written word can be imbued with symbolic power. This awareness is threaded throughout her work, which explores the dense intersectionality of literary and pictorial narratives.

Jinchi achieved a Bachelor of Science in Civil Engineering from George Washington University (1982). Though her studies honed her analytical mind, she ultimately decided to pursue a career in the creative field. Trained as a classical calligrapher in Iran, Pouran went on to study art at UCLA and the Art Students League of New York. Drawing on this varied training, Jinchi developed her own artistic approach. Her attention to methodology stems from a background as a mathematician; her formal approach reflects a creative tension between the rigid control of traditional Islamic calligraphy and the fluid spontaneity of Western abstract painting.

Jinchi's art has been featured internationally in exhibitions in New York, London, Venice, Dusseldorf, Dubai, Jeddah, Shanghai and Tokyo. These include *The Line of March*, The Third Line, Dubai, UAE (2017); *The Blind Owl*, The Third Line, Dubai, UAE (2013); *Dawn, Noon and Night*, Art Projects International, New York, USA (2012); and *Ritual Imprint*, The Third Line, Dubai, UAE (2010).

Her work has also been included in group exhibitions such as *Long, Winding Journeys: Contemporary Art and the Islamic Tradition*, Katonah Museum of Art, New York, USA (2018); *The Great Game*, Iranian Pavilion 56th Venice Biennale, Venice, Italy (2015); *Ravaged Garden*, NYU Art Gallery, New York (2015); *Deceptively Simple*, Art Project International Gallery, New York, USA (2015); *Accented*, Maraya Art Center, Sharjah, UAE (2015); *Artist in Exile: Creativity, Activism and the Diasporic Experience*, Dr. M. T. Geoffrey Yeh Art Gallery, St John's University, Queens, New York, USA (2014); *Persepolis: Word and Image*, The William Benton Museum of Art, University of Connecticut, Storrs, USA (2014); *Calligraffiti: 1984/2013*, Leila Heller Gallery, New York, USA (2013); *New Blue and White*, Museum of Fine Arts, Boston, USA (2013); *Phantoms of Asia*, Asian Art Museum, San Francisco, USA (2012); *Light of the Sufi: Mystical Arts of Islam*, Museum of Fine Arts, Houston, USA (2010); *Light of the Sufi: Mystical Arts of Islam*, Brooklyn Museum, New York, USA (2009), and *Translation/Tarjama*, Queens Museum of Art, New York, USA (2009).

Jinchi's artworks are part of museum collections worldwide, including the Metropolitan Museum of Art, New York; the Brooklyn Museum, New York; Arthur M. Sackler Gallery of the Smithsonian, Washington, DC; Museum of Fine Arts, Houston; the Cincinnati Art Museum; Art Jameel, Dubai; Zayed National Museum, Abu Dhabi; Herbert F. Johnson Museum at Cornell University; the Pratt Institute, New York, Federal Reserve Bank of New York; and Newport Art Museum, Rhode Island.

Jinchi lives and works in New York City.

Author Biographies

Dr. Maryam Ekhtiar is a scholar and specialist in the field of later Persian art and culture. One of her particular areas of expertise is calligraphy. She received her Ph.D. from the Department of Middle Eastern Studies at New York University in 1994 and has worked and taught at various museums and universities in the United States, namely the Brooklyn Museum, New York University and Swarthmore College. She was co-editor of, and contributor to, the catalogue *Royal Persian Paintings: The Qajar Epoch 1785–1925*. She is Associate Curator at the Department of Islamic Art, Metropolitan Museum of Art, and has been working there for roughly fourteen years. She is co-editor of the recent catalogue *Masterpieces from the Department of Islamic Art at the Metropolitan Museum of Art* and *Art of the Islamic World: A Resource for Educators* and has published and lectured extensively in the fields of Islamic art, Iranian art and contemporary art from the Middle East and North Africa. Her book *How to Read the Art of Islamic Calligraphy* is due to be published in November 2018.

Dr. Shiva Balaghi is an independent scholar based in Los Angeles. Balaghi was among the first faculty to introduce the subject of Contemporary Middle Eastern Art at US universities, teaching for nearly two decades at New York University and Brown University. Her curatorial projects include co-curating a retrospective of Iran's leading sculptor Parviz Tanavoli at Wellesley's Davis Museum and curating Ghada Amer's first exhibit in the Arab world in two decades. She has written widely on visual culture for museums such as the Guggenheim, the Fine Arts Museum of San Francisco, and the Andy Warhol Museum and for publications like *Artforum*, *Ibraaz*, and *Hyperallergic*. Her books include *Picturing Iran: Art, Society and Revolution*.

Ben Eastham is a writer and editor based in London. He is founding editor of *The White Review*, associate editor of *ArtReview*, and was associate editor of documenta 14. His writing has appeared in publications including *frieze*, the *London Review of Books*, *The New York Times*, *Mousse*, art-agenda, *The Times Literary Supplement* and elsewhere. He has written catalogue essays for artists including Ed Ruscha, Camille Henrot and John Gerrard. His first book, *My Life as a Work of Art*, co-authored with Katya Tylevich, was published in 2016.

Credits